HUBBELL TRADING POST
NATIONAL HISTORIC SITE

by
David M. Brugge

Photography by
George H. H. Huey

WESTERN NATIONAL PARKS ASSOCIATION
TUCSON, ARIZONA

Copyright 1993 by Western National Parks Association,
Tucson, Arizona

ISBN 1-877856-18-5
Library of Congress Number 92-62158

Edited by Ron Foreman
Book Design by Christina Watkins
Typography by Daniel Rirdan
Printing by Imago
Printed in Thailand

All historic photographs from the Hubbell Collection, National Park Service,
Hubbell Trading Post National Historic Site.

The designer and photographer would like to thank the staff
of Hubbell Trading Post National Historic Site for their
cooperation, in particular curators of the Hubbell Collection,
Ed Chamberlain and Kathy Tabaha, for their assistance with
artifacts and photographs.

Frontispiece—"Ganado, Arizona 1908," oil painting by E.A. Burbank,
Hubbell Collection.

Contents page—Detail above the door to Hubbell Trading Post.

Back cover—The Rug Room, Hubbell Trading Post National Historic Site.

Contents

The old man spoke softly and slowly, but with the self-assurance of one who is used to commanding attention. Even so, there was a sense of urgency in his voice as he told the story of his life and experiences here at Hubbell Trading Post in Ganado, Arizona, in the heart of Navajo country. Don Lorenzo Hubbell knew that this interview with a young writer would be his last.

He wanted the facts to be those he chose to reveal. Like all of us, he tended to omit his sins and mistakes. If his memory was not perfect, the magazine article that J. E. Hogg was to write was even less so. But Hubbell, whom the Navajos affectionately called Naakaii Sání, "Old Mexican," would not live to read it.

Facing Page: Ruin of small Anasazi dwelling on Pueblo Colorado Wash.

There was more to the story of this place than Hubbell could tell, however. The land that he called home had a history much longer than one man's lifetime. Not far from the trading post lay the remains of the homes of earlier occupants, of Navajo hogans dating back almost two centuries and Anasazi pueblos over six centuries old.

Hubbell Trading Post is located in the Valley of the Red House—from the Spanish Pueblo Colorado, "Red Village," and from the Navajo Kin Dah Łichíí, "Red Upon the House." A prehistoric Pueblo Indian ruin, the Red House is still partially standing with massive walls—originally two or three stories tall—reminiscent of the Anasazi great houses at Chaco Canyon. Its Navajo name has been anglicized to Kinlichee, and it has long been a landmark known to travelers through the region.

Tree-ring dates from ceiling beams indicate that the Red House was occupied during the eleventh and twelfth centuries. One kiva was built about A.D. 1085–87, and some of the upper-story rooms were roofed about 1126–36. These dates correlate with the height of development at Chaco Canyon, suggesting that there may have been close ties, or at least trade contacts, with that major center of prehistoric Pueblo life.

Several miles down the Pueblo Colorado Wash is Wide Reeds, or Lók´aahnteel, a pueblo that dates from about 1276, just as the Great Drought of 1276–99 was causing devastation throughout the Colorado Plateau. Wide Reeds was a medium-sized village of perhaps only one story, and home to several families of Indian farmers.

We cannot know what language the people of the Red House or Wide Reeds spoke nor exactly what they believed, but they were part of a wider cultural entity that today we call the Anasazi. They depended on crops of maize, pumpkins, and beans, supplemented by some wild game and edible native plants. Thus, many of their prayers were for rain, to make the vegetation grow, and for the fertility of life.

During the Great Drought the Anasazi left much of their ancient homelands. Their descendants now live in the surviving pueblos at Hopi, Zuni, and along the Rio Grande drainage of New Mexico.

Although the abandonment of all the San Juan drainage, and much of the Little Colorado, came during the Great Drought, archeologists still question whether it was the sole cause of the depopulation of so vast a territory. No firm evidence has been found for competing theories such as epidemic disease, attacks by invading enemies, or simple social disintegration. While one or all of these factors may have been involved, the drought itself seems to have been the primary disaster.

The land remained. The scars of erosion—arroyos, washed slopes, blowouts, and dunes—gradually disappeared when the rains returned. New vegetation spread to hold the runoff, resulting in yet more growth. Animal life followed wherever there were plants to graze, browse, or nibble. But the Pueblo people did not return to live in the Pueblo Colorado Valley. Over a wide area, two millennia or more of cultural development were truncated by the drought. When human beings again took up residence, they brought new ways of life, influenced by the old, but with traditions that grew from other roots.

Sometime after A.D. 1400, perhaps not long after the land had recovered, people speaking a language closely akin to the Athabaskan languages of southwestern Canada began to penetrate the Colorado Plateau. Their descendants, the Navajos and other Apaches, were the first neighbors of the surviving Pueblos identified with any certainty by the early Spanish chroniclers. At first, the Spanish used vague terms such as Querechos and Apaches, neither specifying exactly which tribes or bands they encountered nor just where they were living. By the seventeenth century, the archives leave little doubt that the Navajos themselves were in the country. In time, they became well established. Archeological evidence meshes nicely with this identification, but for reasons that require some explanation.

Anasazi olla, bowl, and yucca sandal, Hubbell Collection.

The people of the northern subarctic regions lived by hunting, fishing, and gathering. Theirs was a harsh land, harsher even than the arid Southwest deserts, where the people learned to live scattered in small family groups or bands, gathering together only when there were seasonal opportunities to amass ample food for a crowd. In the Southwest, their descendants continued to follow this lifeway, one well attuned to the sparse resources of nature in their new home. Even as they learned to grow a few crops, they kept to their old social customs. Families valued their independence and freedom from the restrictions that town life might impose.

The culture they brought with them differed from that of the Pueblos in many ways. They wore tailored clothing of buckskin, built one-room conical hogans as homes, used dogs as pack animals when traveling, and hunted with short, sinew-backed bows that were more powerful than the simple wooden bows of their new neighbors.

Respect for the individual was a central value in their belief system. Lacking the communal organization of the Pueblos, each person was important for the survival of the isolated family groups. Ceremonies were held for the good of specific people—for a girl coming of age, a child struck by illness, or a hunter injured in his work. Agents believed responsible for illness or bad luck were feared. These were powerful spirits of nature, witches, and ghosts, and there were rules of behavior to appease or evade them. Funerals were especially elaborate, designed to prevent the ghost of the deceased from returning to disturb the living.

Their religion mandated a positive, even optimistic, outlook. One's words and thoughts could influence events. Thus, one should always anticipate the best.

On the Colorado Plateau the Navajos occupied much of the San Juan drainage. There was soon an exchange of ideas, knowledge, and skills between them and the Puebloans, sometimes through friendly encounters, other times through war. The Navajos learned to raise corn and squash, but seldom planted beans because their hunters brought home ample meat, the preferred source of protein. The Pueblos learned to make the new kind of bow and began to replace their sandals with moccasins.

Navajos also adapted old ways to their new environment. Fishing was of little consequence in the arid Southwest, but the multi-barbed points used on fish spears in the north proved ideal for arrows that would provide a secure grasp on a prairie dog scooting into its burrow.

By the time Spanish explorers began probing Pueblo country, the Athabaskans had established stable and important systems of trade, alliances, and warfare. Different pueblos had different Apachean bands as trading partners and potential allies. The oldest known Navajo archeological sites have only Hopi pottery as a trade ware, but by the 1580s Navajos were trading at Acoma Pueblo, as well.

After Spanish settlers became established in New Mexico in 1598,

Abandoned old-style hogan.

8

the Pueblo people were subject to foreign rule in their political lives and religious observances. Many Pueblos resented this need to obey God and King. Missionary priests regularly complained that their charges envied the freedom of the surrounding Apachean tribes and that some, wishing to live without the restraints of Christian discipline, fled to join the "common enemy." In 1680 the Pueblos revolted with such success that the Spanish were driven back toward Mexico. They were not permanently expelled, however. In the 1690s Spanish rule was reasserted in New Mexico, and refugees from the reconquest swelled the populations of more remote peoples—the Plains Apaches to the east, the Hopis in the far west, and the Navajos to the west and northwest.

Pueblo refugees changed the Navajo way of life forever, introducing a pastoral tradition that ultimately became the foundation of the Navajo economy. During the first several decades of this change, Pueblo ways were conspicuous in Navajo country. The best known Navajo archeology is of special interest because of its spectacular mixture of Athabaskan and Puebloan features. The introduced architectural ideas led to the development of little stone houses or pueblitos, meaning "small pueblos." Most of these structures were built in a region of northwestern New Mexico that Navajo traditionalists came to call the Dinétah, "Among the Navajos." There, over six decades, the refugees and their descendants were integrated into the Navajo tribe and became founders of numerous Navajo clans. The bitterness of the revolt and reconquest softened with time, and by 1720 peace between Navajos and Spaniards had returned.

Navajo log hogan.

The Dinétah was far to the east of the Pueblo Colorado, on the tributaries of the San Juan River in northwestern New Mexico and extending north into southern Colorado. In the latter half of the eighteenth century, the stress of drought and enemy attacks forced the people of the Dinétah to spread out over a wide territory to the south and west, perhaps joining more purely Apachean bands already living in scattered locales. In the wake of contact with invaders from the Old World, deaths due to new diseases such as smallpox, wars, and disruptions of traditional ways had reduced the population of most tribes considerably. In the Dinétah, there was population growth as the mixed peoples there forged a better adaptation to the challenges they faced. They were welcomed in the areas to which they spread, for they brought solutions to pressing problems.

A few pueblitos and defensive retreats, showing evidence of the Dinétah influence, have been located and studied as far west as Ganado and neighboring communities. Northwest of the Pueblo Colorado is a small crag, where several hogans are sheltered behind a fortified rim. Tree-ring dates cluster from 1757 to 1764. To the south near Wide Ruins is Kinaazini, a two-story pueblito with a cluster of dates from 1755 to 1760. Another pueblito lies to the north near Nazlini with dates from 1751 to 1761. No doubt the Navajos had settled in to stay. They were no longer just the descendants of hunters and gatherers from the northwoods, but could count among their ancestors Pueblos deriving ultimately from the Anasazi. They had become farmers and ranchers as skilled at weaving and riding as they were in the chase and in working leather.

By the 1760s Spanish accounts and maps make specific reference to Navajos along or near the trails to Hopi. Most reports and diaries of the time derive from military encounters after 1773, often in the vicinity of Canyon de Chelly. Less dramatic events received only passing mention, if documented at all. The name Cumaa was mapped in the 1770s, appearing close to present-day Ganado. In the early nineteenth century the name Pueblo Colorado appeared with increasing frequency.

Conflict between Euro-Americans and Navajos escalated gradually but steadily, fueled by mounting grievances on both sides and an inability of either party to gain a decisive victory, even after the United States Army began operations out of Fort Defiance in the 1850s. By 1863 the Pueblo Colorado Valley had gained such prominence that Kit Carson was ordered to establish his headquarters there to launch the last Navajo campaign. He concluded that old Fort Defiance was better suited to his needs, but his forces marched all around the region, from the Pueblo Colorado to the Hopi villages and beyond.

Carson's campaign employed two major tactics. The Navajos were continually harassed, forcing them to be constantly on the move. The initial plan was for the army to do this itself, but Carson apparently understood that a large, slow-moving force would not keep up with the Navajos as they scattered to hide, traveling light. He enlisted the alliance of other tribes: Utes, Apaches, and Pueblos. Privateering expeditions of New Mexicans also joined the chase. All were to be rewarded in the traditional fashion, by being allowed to keep the loot and captives they took, or by payment for all livestock turned over to the army.

Carson's second tactic was a scorched-earth policy designed to destroy the Navajo economy, reducing them to starvation and thus forcing them to surrender to eat. All crops and stored supplies that could be found were confiscated or destroyed, and herds were captured as often as possible. A bumper crop of pinyon pine nuts in the far west gave some relief for those able to reach the country beyond Hopi, but thousands of Navajos found it safer to trust the army than to risk attack by the many small parties of raiders.

Ganado Mucho, ca. 1870.

The grand strategy called for all Navajos to be removed from their own country and exiled to Fort Sumner in eastern New Mexico. There, at a place called Bosque Redondo, or "Round Forest," the Navajos endured great privation for more than four years. In 1868 they signed their final treaty with the United States, which allowed them to return to a part of their homeland.

The Navajo reservation was laid out along lines of latitude and longitude, a rectangle that straddled the then-territorial boundary between Arizona and New Mexico. In the early years the precise location of the boundary was not known, for it was not surveyed. The southern edge was close to Fort Defiance and the northern limit was the southern boundary of Utah and Colorado. This arbitrary description ignored the natural geography and the customary uses the people made of the land. The Pueblo Colorado lay to the southwest of the original treaty reservation, but it was home to many followers of Ganado Mucho, "Much Livestock," known in Navajo as

Tótsohnii Hastiin, "Man of the Big Water Clan."

Along the Pueblo Colorado Wash, homes and farms reappeared.
There were no other settlers to contest the right of the former exiles to their
old territory, even though far beyond the limits of the treaty reservation.
They were a conquered people, and their old tribal structure was in ruins.
Federal supervision was tenuous; the Indian agents at Fort Defiance had
only a handful of helpers, few resources, and a burden of bureaucratic
regulations. Most had such short tenure in the position that they could
learn little about the Navajos, much less manage to use their knowledge.
Still, the Navajos were at last fully a part of recorded history, subject to
the political life of the nation, and poised to become integrated into its
economy as well.

Facing Page: Navajo
weaver with loom in
pinyon pine, ca. 1890.

Non-Navajos soon discovered the inviting Valley of the Red House. The first to settle was Charles Hardison, who had married a Navajo wife at Fort Sumner and began ranching as a member of her family near Kinlichee. For a few years he raised cattle there, but when his marriage did not last he moved away.

Other settlers were less closely connected with the Navajos. Some seem to have come originally with the intention of ranching themselves. Finding the land fully occupied by Navajos, they either left or became traders. Indeed, the term "trading ranch" was often applied to their establishments. Indian trade had a long and convoluted history in North America. Frequently, it was the wealth of the wilderness that was the basis of the exchange. Indian hunters who knew their lands intimately harvested the meat, hides, and furs to barter for the manufactured goods of the Europeans. At times, this commerce was sullied by a trade in captives taken from other tribes and sold as slaves. When unregulated by central governments, there were always Europeans willing to take advantage of those with less worldly experience and more limited military power. But there were also merchants who recognized that their business would be profitable only as long as their customers prospered.

To the north and east, from the sixteenth century into the nineteenth, fur was the prize. French, Dutch, and English interests competed and fought to trade for beaver, otter, mink, and marten while the tribes engaged in similar tactics to control the flow of goods and guns from across the sea. To the southeast, it was deer hides for which English and Spanish contended, while in the more open country of mid-continent, the woolly bison pelts were the major commodity. Farther west, fine thick hides of elk were added to those of bison, deer, and antelope. Along the west coast, Russians sought the fur of sea otters.

Few tribes cultivated or manufactured marketable goods of their own, and those that did often saw Europeans rapidly take over the production of such goods themselves. This was not true in New Mexico, a poor colony that relied on Indian labor for many of its needs. Navajos, despite the disruptions of frequent wars, had become skilled producers of livestock and blankets in a land so harsh that few others cared to challenge their claim.

Game was sparse in Navajo country. Spanish trade for deer and antelope hides soon depleted the supply in colonial times, and Anglo-Americans subsequently trapped out the few beaver. A modest trade with neighboring tribes helped maintain contacts between peoples in need of allies, but had limited economic significance. Only the trade in Navajo blankets could be viewed as more of an economic than a social activity.

The Santa Fe Trail opened to legal trade shortly after Mexico gained independence from Spain, changing more than just the economy of the Southwest. New Mexico, formerly an isolated province largely dependent on limited economic resources to the south, was now the entry port for a flood of manufactured goods from the east. Access to modern weapons made the province a more formidable military power in its dealings with the free tribes, including the Apaches and Navajos.

Navajos competed with settlers for products, land, and political autonomy, which made them less than inviting for trade, especially as compared to tribes that could supply furs, buffalo robes, and slaves. Those would-be traders who sought Navajos as customers typically had been shut out of more lucrative markets because they lacked capital and dealt in stolen goods. Peons hoping to escape their masters and herders willing to sell sheep from flocks under their care (and blame the loss on Navajo raiders) had long played a part in the Navajo trade.

Only when the flow of firearms from the East upset all balance of power did the Navajos awake to the need for more extensive trade connections. The few Anglo-Americans who did get into Navajo country in the 1820s, such as one party of beaver trappers, were warmly welcomed, but they did not regard the tribe as a potential source of valuable trade. Even so, it would be the unique economy of the pastoral Navajos that would ultimately make them one of the most desirable tribes for trade once the wars had ended and the products of hunting, trapping, and raiding could no longer be taken in quantity.

When the United States acquired New Mexico in 1846, permission to trade was given to itinerant merchants who took pack animals loaded with goods into Navajo country. The earliest trader of record appears to be Agustin Lacome, who received a license in January 1853. A later license for six months of trading at various named locations in Navajo country required him to post a bond and authorized him to employ helpers. In 1857 his license was suspended, perhaps for belonging to the wrong political party. Others in the 1850s seem to have alternated between trading as itinerants, using pack animals and wagons to carry their stock, and setting up shop at one of the western pueblos, such as Jemez or Zuni, where Navajos frequently visited.

The only established stores in Navajo country were those of the sutlers such as John E. Weber at Fort Defiance in 1860 and A.W. Kavanaugh at Fort Fauntleroy in 1861.

Devastation of the final wars left the Navajos dependent at first on government largess for survival, but they were not long in re-establishing their former trade contacts. Blankets woven by Navajo women were carried to their tribal neighbors to exchange for food and other needs, while trade in New Mexico was often for the purpose of rebuilding herds.

The first traders to actually settle in Navajo country concentrated on hides and pelts, surplus livestock, and occasional craft products. Trade was sporadic and uncertain. In 1875 a major change provided a firm basis for a steady and continuing trade. William Arny, son of W.F.M. Arny, Navajo agent at that time, began to purchase Navajo wool for shipment to woolen mills in the East. Driven by high demand for wool, trade grew rapidly, attracting new entrepreneurs to the reservation and to many locations in adjacent lands where Navajos had settled. In 1875 Arny shipped sixty thousand pounds of Navajo wool by wagon. Traders shipped out two hundred thousand pounds the following year, and the figure grew to eight hundred thousand pounds by the time the Atchison, Topeka & Santa Fe Railway reached the fringes of Navajo country in 1881.

Contract freight wagon, ca 1906.

Shipping wool and hides out—and groceries, dry goods, and hardware in—required transportation by wagon, even after the railroad arrived. Ox teams were ideal for heavy loads, especially when roads were muddy or snow-covered, but they were very slow, managing to travel only two miles an hour when conditions were good. Horses and mules were faster, and by 1900 they had entirely supplanted oxen. Hay, alfalfa, and range grass provided fuel for all.

Trading ranches metamorphosed into true trading posts, and would-be ranchers became the inadvertent owners of mercantile establishments. Men whose skills lay more in business soon arrived, but most lasted only a few months, or at most a few years. Some were lured by the myth of hidden gold deposits in Navajo country, and their real purpose was not to trade, but to surreptitiously locate this mysterious wealth. In addition, they were as vulnerable to political tides as were the government agents, one of whom was said to have been appointed to oversee the Navajo Tribe "because he is a Republican and he put up his money like a man during the last election."

In at least some cases, traders with wagons and tents set up business in various locations until a site favorable for trade was found, then built small stores. Few planned to stay permanently in Navajo country. Many intended to get rich quick by cornering the market for wool, blankets, or some other tempting product, then moving away to live the life of luxury among their own people.

With the arrival of the railroad, trading posts proliferated. Off-reservation posts outnumbered those on the reservation by four to one. Avoidance of government regulations was only one reason for this. The reservation was still relatively small and many Navajos lived outside its boundaries on the public domain. In addition, the railroad in the south, and the San Juan River in the north, provided natural corridors for locating posts. Navajos were well-supplied with horses and willing to travel to find the best prices, but over time increasing competition forced more traders to locate in the interior of Navajo country. Ultimately, the off-reservation traders, trying to preserve their markets, gave valuable support to Navajo requests for more land.

In the Valley of the Red House, there was apparently some kind of settlement by 1871. Charles Crary was reported trading at present-day Ganado that year. Meanwhile, William Leonard was working as a trading post clerk at Fort Defiance. Leonard would soon go into business, acquire Crary's store, and station a clerk there, most likely Barney Williams. Elsewhere in Navajo country John Lorenzo Hubbell, destined to become the major trader at Ganado, was also learning the skills necessary to operate a Navajo trading post.

Hubbell was born in 1853 in Pajarito, New Mexico, and grew up in a bilingual and bicultural family during a time of dramatic and historic events. His father, James Hubbell, was a Connecticut Yankee who had come to New Mexico as a soldier in 1846. His mother, Juliana Gutiérrez, was the granddaughter of one of the first governors of New Mexico under Mexican rule. As a boy, Hubbell saw the Confederate invasion of the

21

territory and the ultimate victory of United States forces, in which his father and uncles served. His uncle and namesake, John Hubbell, perished in that conflict. The Indian wars were still in progress throughout his boyhood, as well. Another uncle, Charles Hubbell, took part in the Carson Campaign, as a member of a column of troops that marched through Canyon del Muerto in 1863 and as commander of an escort for Navajos on their way to Fort Sumner.

Literate in both English and Spanish, Hubbell obtained early experience in business affairs working for the Albuquerque Post Office and for his father, whose military connections had perhaps helped him secure the contract to deliver hay to Fort Wingate. Local Navajos were hired to cut native grass at places from which it could be most easily hauled by wagon to the fort. It is probable that young John Lorenzo, still in his teens, began to learn the Navajo language then from the Indians his father employed.

He also gained experience clerking for pioneer traders in Navajo country, including a post at Fort Wingate and at a store in the Mormon settlement of Kanab, Utah. In later life, he would often entertain visitors with a story about fleeing Kanab with a bullet wound from an altercation about which he provided no details, and wandering wounded in the wilderness until he was rescued by a Paiute family, who nursed him back to health. He loved to indulge in romantic tales of his youth, more it would seem to entertain his listeners than to enhance his own stature. Something of the sort that he described probably happened, but the truth may be a bit more prosaic than the story he spun for visitors. In any case, he traveled widely for his time and met many prominent people in the region.

Hubbell was employed at the Navajo Agency at Fort Defiance in 1874 when news of the killing of three young Navajos in Utah reached Navajo agent Arny. Arny, a Presbyterian, favored those with connections to that church, and Hubbell, although raised a Catholic, had attended a Presbyterian school in Santa Fe. Arny assigned the bilingual Hubbell to accompany Navajo clan leader Ganado Mucho from the Pueblo Colorado on a mission to Utah to investigate the incident and to attempt to settle differences between the Mormons and the Navajos. The Navajos believed, erroneously according to the Mormons, that the people who had killed their men were Mormons, and they demanded reparations. The dispute dragged on for years.

In 1875 Arny was driven from his agency by Navajo headmen angered by his policies. Hubbell remained an agency employee, but apparently began trading in the Pueblo Colorado as early as 1876. He may not have been entirely welcome there at first. He later told a story of being threatened with death until a Navajo headman came to his rescue. Versions of the tale have him tied variously to a wagon wheel or a mesquite tree (a species that does not grow in the Pueblo Colorado area), and credits either Ganado Mucho or Ganado Mucho's son, Many Horses, with saving his life. Among other things, he credited his acceptance to having helped the Navajos of the area during a smallpox epidemic, as he had acquired immunity to the disease as a child. Obviously, these early years are clouded in folklore and legend, the frontier tradition of tall tales, and the artistic license of popular writing.

Not until 1878 does a clear picture of affairs in the Pueblo Colorado emerge in the historical record. That year there was a widespread witch scare among the Navajos that had strong political undercurrents. Hastiin Biwosi, "Mr. Shoulder," was executed by followers of Ganado Mucho near the Pueblo Colorado. He had been a signer of the final treaty, and in 1878 he was headman at Canyon de Chelly. The violence frightened settlers living in the vicinity, who feared an outbreak of warfare. Hubbell's younger brother, Charlie, was operating a trading post just south of Ganado Lake. He wrote from there to Pueblo Colorado area trader William Leonard, pleading for his assistance, first for a gun and ammunition and then for troops. Only in closing did he report the death of Biwosi.

Troops were sent to the Pueblo Colorado, accompanied by the Navajo agent. They arrived too late to prevent the killing of some alleged witches, but they did save two medicine men who were being held captive by the local Navajos. Their presence may have helped avert a clash between

Watercolor of the Leonard Buildings by Marion K. Wachtel, ca. 1905, Hubbell Collection.

the people of the Canyon de Chelly area and those of the Pueblo Colorado.

When this incident occured, Hubbell was actually in New Mexico at a place he called Navajo City, near the home of Manuelito, Ganado Mucho's counterpart in the eastern Navajo country. At Manuelito's request, he wrote to the commanding officer at Fort Wingate to report similar troubles among Navajos living farther north. Hubbell served as interpreter for troops sent to restore peace and rescue other medicine men threatened with execution. The officer who led the troops commended Hubbell for his services.

Hubbell probably had a financial interest in the business that his brother Charlie operated south of Ganado Lake. According to various accounts, one of the presumed witches was killed in the doorway of the trading post, an event that doomed the business there. In order not to lose the Navajos' trade entirely, Hubbell purchased Leonard's store on the Pueblo

Colorado. The property consisted of several structures located north of the eventual Hubbell home, dubbed "the Leonard Buildings." These original, rather primitive structures, built of stone and a wood-lattice-and-mud mixture called jacal (hah-CALL), were razed in the 1920s.

In 1880 the Pueblo Colorado area was added to the Navajo Reservation, and the legal status of the land on which Hubbell's Ganado trading post was located would remain in doubt for many years. He was apparently an absentee owner initially, because that same year he received a license to trade in Manuelito's community in New Mexico. Hubbell also had a store and rented rooms in St. Johns, Arizona, south of the reservation. There he was said to be courting "the most beautiful woman in Northern Arizona," no doubt Lina Rubí, daughter of a couple from Cebolleta, New Mexico, who were among the first settlers of St. Johns.

In the 1880s Hubbell began to be active in politics. As a New Mexican of half-Hispanic ancestry, he soon was involved in helping defend the interest of the Hispanic settlers of St. Johns in their competition with the Mormons. As sheriff, he sided with Hispanic sheepmen against lawless Texas cattlemen who came into the area. In 1892 he was elected to the territorial House of Representatives. He represented his district in the Arizona Legislature for many terms, and is credited by some Mormon writers with helping to resolve differences between Mormon and Hispanic peoples.

Hubbell's life during the 1880s was centered as much at St. Johns as at the Ganado trading post. It was probably then that he acquired the honorific title of "Don" for his leadership in the local Hispanic community. He also expanded into sheep ranching briefly. He and Lina became the parents of two girls, Adela and Barbara, the beginnings of a family that would spur Don Lorenzo to expand his enterprises rather than settle down in a single community. He did give up his addiction to gambling when Doña Lina reportedly threatened to leave him after he had lost thirty thousand dollars in one card game.

In 1883 the two rooms now used as office and rug room at the

Barbara (left) and Adela Hubbell, ca. 1886.

present Hubbell Trading Post were built. This was the first substantial stone building erected and an indication of Don Lorenzo's concern for permanent and well-built facilities. By then at Ganado, Don Lorenzo had almost certainly acquired the Navajo name Nák'ee Sinilí, "Eyeglasses," by which he was known for many years.

C.N. Cotton Building, Gallup, New Mexico, ca 1890.

Facing Page: Hubbell Trading Post wareroom, J. L. Hubbell seated on sack of wool (left), ca. 1885.

The following year he formed a partnership with C. N. Cotton, who had come west to work as a telegraph operator for the railroad. As full of energy and enthusiasm as Don Lorenzo, Cotton had eastern connections and a business aptitude that made him an ideal partner. Cotton also received a Navajo appellation, Hastiin Béésh Bewoo'í, "Mr. Metaltooth," for his gold-capped teeth. He is remembered by many older Navajos as a friendly and affable man. In 1885 Cotton bought out Hubbell's remaining interest in the Ganado store, but they remained friends and partners in other undertakings.

Then as now, businessmen tended to be circumspect in their relationships, partly to gain and maintain advantage in business dealings, but also out of habit. Many casual visitors learned too little and assumed too much, as is evident in this account by Herbert Welsh, who investigated Indian affairs in the Southwest for the Indian Rights Association in 1884.

> We passed our first night at the Trading Ranch of Messrs. Hubbell and Pillsbury, to whose kindness and hospitality we are much indebted. Lorenzo Hubbell is an older brother of the Mr. Hubbell whose name occurs earlier in my report. He is engaged in a successful business as a trader with the Indians. We found him most courteous and agreeable, and possessing a clear and intelligent mind. His home is in St. Johns . . .

Pillsbury, a distinctly minor character in the story, was merely a hired clerk. The nature of the Hubbell-Cotton business relationship is similarly

obscure. We know little of how they worked together, but it is apparent that they cooperated closely and had mutual interests.

Cotton soon began an ambitious marketing effort to promote greater sales of Navajo products. He found a market among Italian immigrants in New York City for the pinyon nuts that the Navajos harvested, for they were much like the pine nuts of the Mediterranean. He wrote to merchants in mining towns to offer Navajo blankets for sale, asserting that they would make ideal camp blankets for miners and prospectors. In one such letter, he added as an afterthought that they could also be used as rugs. The Navajo rug was yet a gleam in the eyes of a trader, but this passing remark would prove prophetic.

Cotton also searched diligently for reliable sources of products desired by Navajos, such as high-quality turquoise and real Mediterranean red coral beads like the Spanish once imported.

By 1886 Cotton and Hubbell were buying wool in quantity from the Navajos—Cotton at Ganado and Hubbell perhaps at the same place. Charlie Hubbell, clerking for Cotton at a post in Blue Canyon west of the Hopi villages, was also buying wool. By the middle of May that year, they had purchased over forty thousand pounds.

Cotton and Don Lorenzo would remain close friends throughout their lives, but Cotton's deep immersion in business and Don Lorenzo's wide ranging interests led them in different directions. Sometime in the 1880s, Cotton conceived the idea of a wholesale house that would cater to the special needs of traders in Navajo country. He moved his family to Gallup, New Mexico, and before the decade was out he had built a large warehouse there to supply traders with all the goods Navajos wanted and to handle Navajo products that had found a market in the outside world.

Hubbell sold his store in St. Johns in 1887, but it is unclear whether he continued to maintain a primary residence there. Meanwhile, he and Doña Lina had another child, Lorenzo, Jr., who would grow up to follow his father's lead in fact as well as in name, as a trader among both the Navajos and the Hopis.

In 1889 the large room used for the Ganado store and the wareroom were added to the two rooms built in 1883. The size of these additions is indicative of a prosperous and growing business. Although Cotton still owned the post, the building style, especially that of the store, hints at participation by Hubbell. It may well be that he recruited skilled builders from among his wife's relatives in St. Johns to supervise the work.

Cotton filed the first recorded homestead claim for 160 acres encompassing the Ganado property in 1890, but the request was denied because the site was by then within the expanded Navajo Reservation and

Hubbell family portrait, ca. 1895. Don Lorenzo, Barbara, Adela, and Dona Lina; Lorenzo, Jr. and Roman.

had not been surveyed. He petitioned the Commissioner of Indian Affairs to have the trading post site excepted from the reservation, and a subsequent inquiry from Washington elicited a favorable recommendation from the agent at Fort Defiance. The Commissioner nonetheless found no authority to make an exception in the order that created the reservation extension, so the Department of the Interior set the land aside pending Congressional action that would address the rights of settlers. Cotton accepted the department order as sufficient for the moment.

Facing Page: Old freight wagon in barnyard.

In 1895 Cotton sold the Ganado post back to Don Lorenzo, who had probably managed the store since Cotton's move to Gallup. The next attempt to obtain full title began in 1899. With the support of Cotton, a

Barn and corrals at Hubbell Trading Post, ca. 1909.

leading Indian rights advocate, the Navajo agent, the Governor of Arizona, and others, Hubbell asked that he be given title to the land. Congress passed a bill excepting lands within the extension that were claimed by actual settlers. Hubbell, the only claimant, filed a homestead entry. He finally received his patent to the land in 1908, although a new patent was required in 1917 to correct errors in the original survey.

The Hubbells meanwhile had a second son, Roman. Don Lorenzo brought the family to live at Ganado only during the summer months, for the children attended school the rest of the year. He ultimately acquired homes in Gallup and Albuquerque as well as St. Johns, and his family had ample choice of residence and schools while he ran the business at Ganado.

Through the 1890s his living quarters at the trading post were in the old Leonard Buildings, two aging jacal structures that were doubtless often plagued by cold drafts and leaky roofs. An adobe room with an attached root cellar was built about 1897 or 1898 behind the trading post, but its function during this period is not at all clear. Today, it is the dining room of the Hubbell house.

Cotton had contracted freight companies to haul both merchandise to be sold at the store and wool and hides destined for market. Hubbell, with numerous relatives needing jobs and a more operational interest in the business, began to buy wagons and to employ teamsters. Economic conditions and drought adversely affected the Navajo economy in the 1890s. It may be that Hubbell found it necessary to reduce expenses, and establishing a freighting business was one way of doing so. Soon he was hauling goods for other traders and the government as well. Late in the decade, he built a massive stone barn that functioned as a stable for his draft animals rather than as shelter for cattle.

Hubbell may already have begun small-scale farming on part of the 160 acres that would ultimately be recognized as his homestead. Crops included vegetables, melons, and fruit that were sold in the store or consumed by personnel. His main plantings were rye, hay, and alfalfa for his horses and mules. The blacksmith shop may have been part of the stables at an early date also, providing in-house repairs of equipment and shoes for the oxen, mules, and horses that literally supplied horsepower for his enterprises. Bread was baked for both store and staff, as well as family when they were present.

His economizing was based on a philosophy of self-sufficiency and led to investment in improvements and equipment that would help increase profits while cutting costs. He was also able to employ relatives and Navajo customers during a difficult period. This local version of the old Hispanic patron system, adapted to a reservation milieu, became institutionalized in his business, giving it a feudalistic character that was unique.

Early efforts of Hubbell and Cotton to create a chain of trading posts foundered in the political quagmire of licensing, both at Blue Canyon and in a short-lived post at Chinle that was soon taken over by a competitor for the trading license issued in Washington. In the 1890s, however, Hubbell was again ready to apply his talent to the building of a trading empire. One of his first outliers was a post at Cornfields, about ten miles down the wash from his home post at Ganado. By 1896 Charles Cousins was managing the post, and it was to remain in Hubbell ownership for many years.

Competitors came and went. Thomas Keam, the English gentleman trader for whom Keams Canyon is named, endured through the end of the century. His reputation blended with that of Don Lorenzo as a popularizer of Navajo and Hopi crafts. J.B. Moore bought the post at Crystal in 1897 and Richard Wetherill, under the auspices of the Hyde Exploring Expedition, began a trading operation in Chaco Canyon in 1898. Moore, like Hubbell and Cotton, exerted strong influence on Navajo weaving that not only raised the quality of the fabrics but also helped to bring about the shift from blankets to rugs. Wetherill, whose own trading empire grew rapidly, was initially regarded by Hubbell as a dangerous competitor, but withdrawal of the Hyde brothers' financing led to the rapid decline of the Wetherill fortunes.

By the turn of the century Hubbell had set a course that he would follow for the remainder of his career. It would lead him into a far wider variety of undertakings than he could have imagined as a young man, nearly three decades earlier.

The Leonard Buildings, ca. 1895. Don Lorenzo stands under tree, Many Horses wears serape.

33

Hubbell's prosperity did not develop in a vacuum. His enterprising spirit made it possible, but the trading business itself was maturing. In 1883 more than 1.3 million pounds of Navajo wool were purchased by the traders, plus up to three hundred thousand sheep pelts and one hundred thousand goat hides. Navajo herds were increasing and the people were able to eat mutton regularly. It was a time of prosperity and rising expectations for the traders and their customers.

Trading methods were refined during this period. Competition led the traders to court their customers in many ways, some quite obvious and some perhaps a bit devious. Most Navajos visited a trading post infrequently, traveling long distances. Hospitality was expected. Lunch snacks such as canned tomatoes and crackers were regularly provided, along with the "makings" for cigarettes. Children were often treated to candy. Many trading posts had a hogan where customers from remote homes could spend the night. Overnight accommodations included provisions for dinner.

35

Hubbell became known among the Navajos for his hospitality and generosity. He may well have initiated many of the small courtesies such as snacks and tobacco that became so much a part of the business. He knew how to dispense his gifts in a friendly way that added to his reputation, joking in Navajo to maintain a cordial atmosphere for his customers. Navajos came from as far as Navajo Mountain on horseback and by wagon to trade with him.

Wealthy stockmen, whose wool clip might make the difference between a good season and a bad one for the trader, received special attention. Hubbell might give the big owner a better price per pound for his wool than for the small lots brought in by poorer customers. He would also go to great lengths to ensure that any jewelry desired by his more prominent customers was of the best turquoise or coral available.

Facing Page: Chicken pull at Ganado, ca. 1913.

Traders began taking pawn before the turn of the century. The value of silver jewelry as collateral against which loans could be made was a stimulus to the craft. Both agents and traders brought Hispanic smiths into Navajo country to help instruct Navajo smiths in silver and iron work. Cotton and Hubbell were among those who did so, and Ganado early on became a center for silver work.

It was not easy to advertise among the Navajos, who did not read newspapers. Two ways were found that meshed well with the native culture, however.

Major Navajo ceremonies attract large crowds. At Enemyway, held in the summer, young couples perform the nightly Squaw Dance, as it is called in English. The great winter ceremonies include Nightway, at which public ritual dancing by the Yeibichai is performed, and Mountainway, where the Fire Dance, Feather Dance, and other dramatic displays take place. Traders helped defray the cost of the ceremonies, ensuring that they would be held close to their posts. While this carried the risk of disapproval by missionaries and Federal agents, it gained the goodwill of their Navajo neighbors and brought potential customers from far afield.

Less controversial, but perhaps more expensive since the trader

bore the entire cost, were "chicken pulls," the Navajo version of rodeos. These could be held right at the trading post, but required the trader to feed all comers and put up prizes for races and other contests. The name derives from an old Spanish sport in which a chicken was buried in the sand, with only its head above the ground. Riders on horses running at full gallop competed to grab the chicken. The successful contestant then had to out-race all the rest to keep his trophy, which was usually torn to pieces in the melee. Traders came to substitute a sack of coins for a chicken. Hubbell's chicken pulls were among the best attended.

Young Navajo women attending chicken pull, ca. 1913.

Navajo burial customs involved restrictions on those who actually took a body to its final resting place. The people soon learned that non-Indians, who did not have to follow these complex observances, could perform burial duties much more easily than could Navajo tribesmen. In communities where traders were the only non-Navajos, they often were obliged to provide this service, however reluctantly.

Currency was scarce in Navajo country. One solution was to issue seco, or "tin money." These were actually stamped in brass or aluminum in denominations ranging from five cents to one dollar, with a few as high as five dollars. Tin money was normally good only at the trading post where it was given out, but friendly traders might accept each other's tin and exchange it periodically. Most tin went into circulation through the purchase of goods from the Navajos. Customers often received tin as change when they purchased less value than their own goods were worth. Some Navajo employees received tin as wages.

Traders were sometimes more generous with tin than they were with silver currency, in which case it could work to the customer's advantage. Among other uses, it could be used to pay a Navajo singer or medicine man for a curing ritual, and was accepted in the mission collection plate. In at least one case, an old Navajo is said to have buried a large tin treasure. Unfortunately, he never told his relatives where he planted his hoard of tokens, and they could never find them after he died.

Hubbell used tin money for many years, ordering it from suppliers in the Midwest. Long after it was no longer circulated, the store would honor any that a Navajo brought in to spend.

The token system served as a stimulus to economic activity, but it tended to tie recipients to a particular post or chain of posts, and could be subject to abuse. The government periodically tried to eliminate the use of tin money, but off-reservation traders continued the practice long after most reservation posts had given it up. As cash became more widely circulated and Navajos learned to accept paper money more readily, the custom faded of its own accord.

Traders became the most frequently consulted intermediaries between the dominant society and the Navajo communities they served. Government officials relied on them to disseminate news of changes in federal policies, contact specific people in the community, help recruit students for the Indian schools, and support official programs. Hubbell was scrupulous in his dealings with government officials. He had respect for the law, but he also seemed to feel that working with federal authorities was a matter of patriotism, as his letters of advice to his sons indicate.

Most hiring of Navajos for off-reservation work was done through the traders. Doubtless as a result of the traders' influence, Hubbell's grandson, Hubbell Parker, became the Santa Fe Railway's liaison with Navajo employees. Most new arrivals in a Navajo community, whether short-term visitors or people whose business brought them for a lengthy stay, usually contacted the trader first and depended on his advice and influence with the local people. Navajos, on the other hand, relied upon the trader for information and help when dealing with strangers or when leaving to work outside Navajo country. Traders also read letters to older Navajos and wrote replies for them.

Elderly Navajo man at Hubbell Trading Post, ca. 1905.

This status as intermediary between two cultures gave traders a great deal of power in a community. They sometimes resented outsiders who dealt independently with "their Indians," and could often be the deciding influence in whether the people accepted government programs. Although respected local Navajo leaders generally settled internal disputes within a community, traders were sometimes consulted, as well, perhaps by those who felt the headman's decision was unjust.

Commerce smooths out the ups and downs of nature—the effects of droughts, locusts, floods, and hard winters. It also introduces its own ups and downs. The Panic of 1893 initiated a national depression that coincided with losses due to storms and drought in Navajo country. The hardships persisted until the turn of the century, and many trading posts went out of business. Craft work, especially weaving, increased dramatically as families tried to maximize the value of what they had to sell. During this period annual fall lamb sales became important. Poor people had to sell their lambs to buy foods that would last through the winter. Wheat flour began to replace corn as the major element in the diet of many families.

Prosperity returned slowly as herds recovered from previous losses. The sale of livestock became commercialized. Traders at first drove herds on foot to the railroad, hiring Navajo herders to help with the long trek. In time, trucks replaced the trail drive. Many Navajos were becoming commercial ranchers rather than subsistence herders, and before the turn of the century agents warned that the range was becoming crowded and overgrazed. Some families could not control sufficient acreage to raise even a subsistence herd. A vigorous national economy, however, supported a good market for crafts and created jobs for some of the growing population. Improved sanitation

Wool-laden wagons in front of Hubbell Trading Post, ca. 1906.

and a good diet contributed to an extraordinary population growth rate that the government seemed to ignore.

People who harbored the stereotype of the "vanishing redman" did not take seriously reports of increasing population among the Navajos. There was never enough money appropriated for schools for Navajo children, while funds for other governmental services also consistently fell short of the need.

Hubbell corral in the spring of 1906.

The new century brought hope and prosperity to traders and Indians alike. The ending of economic hard times released pent up energy. Hubbell, with his self-sufficient operation, was well prepared to benefit from the improved business climate.

This new prosperity was evident in the construction of the major portion of the large adobe house that in some ways resembled Hubbell's boyhood home in Pajarito. The logs that formed the vigas, or roof beams, of the hall and the five flanking bedrooms were cut in the forest about ten miles east of Ganado during the summer of 1901. Transporting the logs to Ganado must have been a challenge for Hubbell's teamsters, for it meant long hours and hard work on a route that crossed sandy arroyos and steep slopes. The beams were probably seasoned through the winter, for Hubbell moved into the house early in 1902, on the same day that Stewart Culin arrived on a trip to collect artifacts for the Brooklyn Museum.

Photographs taken by Ben Wittick shortly after show a hall with few and simple furnishings, but amply decorated with baskets and other Indian crafts on the walls and

Navajo rugs on the floor. Hubbell may have sold or given away some of these items. Indeed, many were replaced with more elegant decor in later years.

Don Lorenzo at home, ca. 1903.

Don Lorenzo's personality set the tone for the hall, a strong reflection that his family was absent during most of the year. Visitors today sometimes comment on the "masculine" quality of the furnishings. The house became a showplace, a well-set stage upon which he could royally entertain guests from all walks of life with food, drink, good conversation, and music. The image he projected within this baronial mansion would be an asset in both business and politics.

It would be easy to mistake Don Lorenzo's home as nothing more than a facade for furthering his ambitions, but in a deeper sense it was a projection of both his personality and heritage. He was a strong-willed and forceful individual with an ever-restless curiosity and drive. Don Lorenzo epitomized the Spanish traditions of patriarchal family structure and free hospitality. But an even stronger basis for the accumulation of so many artifacts of classical Euro-American culture was the need to preserve a refuge in the midst of an alien culture. His guests and those on his staff with whom he socialized were Hispanic and Anglo-Americans, Germans, Argentineans, Christians, and Jews. Indians seldom entered except as servants, participating minimally in social events in the house.

Indians were not purposely excluded. Navajo society and Euro-American society were two very different worlds separated by language, religious belief, manners, and customs so divergent that only by special effort or in superficial ways could Navajos and non-Navajos join in social affairs. There were too many ways in which outsiders from either world could inadvertently give offense or feel they did not belong. Hubbell strongly supported racial equality, women's rights, and religious tolerance. He also knew instinctively the practical limits of intercultural relationships, and the dangers of culture shock. Despite the compartmentalization of activities at Ganado, his sons grew up with the accepting and liberal attitudes of their father.

With the exception of Navajo rugs and blankets, Indian crafts in the Hubbell home were simply decorative. Objects to be used, from chairs and tables to books and phonograph records, were the products of distant factories. Here on long and lonely winter evenings Hubbell could read, write, or simply sit and enjoy his solitude in culturally familiar surroundings when he did not have guests or a compatible employee with whom to chat. In the summer, his children and grandchildren were exposed to the best that his cultural traditions could supply in terms of art, music, literature, and travelers with diverting tales of the wider world.

Don Lorenzo and Navajo employees, ca. 1906.

The business world was very much the opposite. Navajo customers were welcomed and Navajo employees were essential to success. The Navajo language was the *lingua franca* of trade. Hubbell himself spoke fluent, if sometimes lopsided, Navajo, whether indulging in jokes or serious bargaining, giving instruction and encouragement to weavers and stockmen to help improve their production and products, trying to explain the vagaries of federal regulations that changed with each new agent and each change of the national administration, or directing his Navajo workers. He recorded Navajo words at times with a mixture of English and Spanish conventions for spelling, but made no effort to write texts in Navajo.

His interests in his Navajo neighbors began with what would be best for his business. He conducted himself much like a feudal Spanish lord

of the manor. While not unique, his views were not shared by all traders. Still, they or something like them were the basis for traders who were successful over the long term.

> The first duty of an Indian trader, in my belief, is to look after the material welfare of his neighbors; to advise them to produce that which their natural inclinations and talent best adapts them; to treat them honestly and insist upon getting the same treatment from them . . . to find a market for their production of same, and advise them which commands the best price. This does not mean that the trader should forget that he is to see that he makes a fair profit for himself, for whatever would injure him would naturally injure those with whom he comes in contact.

Paternalistic, but not patronizing, Don Lorenzo's philosophy fit the conditions of the time, as the Navajo people groped for solutions in a world very different from that in which their cultural traditions had been formed. History, culture, and language united the Navajos and set them apart. They were as apt to criticize and joke about the aliens in their midst as the intruders were to view the Navajos as strange.

Navajos are an optimistic people with an adventurous spirit and a fine sense of humor, a people who have long taken a pragmatic view of the world. The heroes and heroines of their traditions went forth to contend with the primal forces of the universe and with the gods themselves, and returned to their people with curing ceremonies and blessings to bestow long life and happiness. Wavering government policies, swings in the market for sheep and wool, missionaries with diverse opinions about the white man's God, and an array of inventions and techniques have presented new opportunities as well as challenges.

Hubbell may not have fully appreciated the Navajos' potential, but he was ever willing to give promising young Navajos opportunities in his

Facing Page: The living room of the Hubbell home.

47

business operations. He hired Navajos to carry the mail, help plant his fields, erect his buildings, freight his wagonloads of merchandise, and, ultimately, clerk in and manage some of his stores.

Hubbell was a strong advocate of education, and gave part of his land at Ganado to the Navajo community as a place to build a Bureau of Indian Affairs school. Just after the turn of the century Hubbell also offered to help the Presbyterians establish a mission at Ganado. He had tried, and failed, to persuade the Franciscan missionaries at St. Michaels, Arizona, to expand their work to his location. His liberal attitudes toward religion were notable for his time.

Hubbell Trading Post compound from Hubbell Hill, ca. 1906.

Facing Page: Hubbell Trading Post National Historic Site.

He invited the first missionary and his wife to stay with him until they became established. Their stay lasted for about a year as the first buildings went up on land that Hubbell had helped them acquire from a Navajo family. His interest, it is said, was as much in the establishment of a mission school as in the Christianization of the Navajos, but his generosity was in keeping with his own nature. The missionary's wife was a school teacher, and she began teaching students in Hubbell's dining room in the Leonard Buildings. Hubbell's daughters Adela and Barbara helped at the Sunday services by playing the piano and organ.

Hubbell began to develop his irrigation system sometime around the turn of the century, perhaps as a result of his homestead claim. The first ditch, built entirely with Hubbell's money, diverted water from the Pueblo Colorado Wash to a holding reservoir, and then to his fields. In 1913 Hubbell granted his ditch to the government in exchange for a water right in the new federal irrigation system that would serve local Navajos.

Hubbell worked closely with H. F. Robinson, an engineer assigned by the Indian Irrigation Service to oversee an area that included Ganado. Previous surveys had identified the Pueblo Colorado as an ideal place for an irrigation project. The plan was to divert the wash into a small natural lake, which would be dammed to increase its capacity for storage. Hubbell's political influence was crucial to getting money appropriated in Congress.

Once construction began in 1913, Robinson was the key person, but Hubbell supported the project by hosting Irrigation Service personnel and freighting materials from Gallup. He also hired a young, well-educated Navajo, David Hubbard, to manage the Dam Store that supplied the workers. He probably played a role in recruiting Navajo workers as well. Work was done by hand or using teams of horses and mules supplied by Hubbell and his Navajo neighbors.

The irrigation system suffered severe damage from floods and required major repairs in 1914, 1916, and 1917, and minor repairs thereafter. An unprecedented series of storms in 1923 caused repeated damage, but the system survived and was quickly put back into serviceable condition.

At the same time, the government tried to decide how to assign land and water rights. Hubbell's rights to water derived from his initial development and his land patent. The Presbyterian mission wanted both land and water rights to teach modern farming methods at the mission school. Even the Bureau of Indian Affairs claimed 274 acres of irrigated land for a proposed school, which was never built. The Navajos could find no one willing to claim authority to assign them their farms. As late as 1918, Robinson complained that the Navajos had "less than 40 acres" under cultivation.

It took the threat of loss of water rights to Arizona to bring action. Robinson raised the warning in 1920. The following year, the agent asked for applications for farms and "was besieged with requests from the Indians." By 1922 Navajos had 110 acres planted, having cleared and leveled their fields and dug the lateral ditches themselves. Most of the farms were small, usually subsistence plots of a few acres of corn, squash, and melons. By 1931 there were seven hundred acres cultivated with a greater variety of crops, including hay, oats, and other vegetables, along with the more traditional produce.

Success varied from year to year. Some seasons failed to yield adequate moisture even with the irrigation system, and some years there were floods that damaged both crops and the irrigation works. The Bureau of Indian Affairs lost interest in the project, even though it had a very good record for its size in terms of the value of crops harvested. Income from farming came to represent a smaller portion of total tribal income, and small projects fell steadily lower in federal priorities. Finally, in the 1950s, appropriations ceased entirely. Gradually, the irrigation system fell into disrepair and then into disuse.

The irrigation project adversely affected the people at Cornfields, downstream from Ganado, who no longer received as much water for their floodwater farms. Arroyo cutting may have been partly to blame for their loss, and precipitation in semi-arid Navajo country was as erratic as it had been in the time of the Anasazi. Still, they tended to place all blame on the dam beneficiaries upstream.

Failure of agriculture in the undependable climate of the reservation was a serious, but not fatal, loss. The Navajos had learned to relegate farming to a secondary place in their lives, to take advantage of opportunities to plant when and where moisture permitted, and to turn their attention to other means of survival.

Hubbell began to acquire new trading posts during this era of prosperity. One of the earliest was the Keams Canyon business, purchased by Lorenzo, Jr., in 1902, probably with his father's assistance. Another important addition to the family holdings was a post at Chinle, built by Don Lorenzo in 1900 on the small rise where the Navajo tribal police station now stands. The

Don Lorenzo's office, ca. 1906.

second floor of this building consisted of guest rooms, Hubbell's intention being to profit from an expected influx of tourists to visit Canyon de Chelly. Bad roads were still an obstacle to tourist travel, and his investment proved to be premature. He also owned the Black Mountain, Nazlini, Oraibi, and Cedar Springs posts in Arizona, the Piñon Springs post south of Gallup in New Mexico, and a store in Gallup that catered to the Navajo trade.

It is not possible to date all of the posts that were owned, nor to be certain in some cases whether Don Lorenzo or Lorenzo, Jr., was the owner. There is even some confusion as to the location of certain posts. One store was at a place called Mud Springs, a mysterious name that does not seem to have survived in common usage.

Arizona posts owned by Lorenzo, Jr., but often attributed to his father, include Piñon, Big Mountain, Dinnebito, Na-ah-tee, Sand Springs

Keams Canyon Trading Post, ca. 1906.

and Marble Canyon. In addition, he bought the store and wholesale house in Winslow from the Richardsons in about 1920. He acquired the Oraibi post from his father in 1918 in exchange for the Keams Canyon business, which Don Lorenzo used to pay off a debt to Cotton.

For Don Lorenzo the Ganado post was home, the headquarters for his business. His freighting operation supplied his outlying posts from there, while he regularly toured the posts, at first by wagon and later by automobile. He never learned to drive, so he had drivers for these visits. He would travel day and night, sleeping in the car between inspections at the stores, and wearing out the drivers, who sometimes would replace each other on the way.

His mail contracts supplemented his freight lines, providing an additional means of communication with his stores and of transportation for goods. It is said that he shipped apples from his orchards near Farmington, on the San Juan River in New Mexico, by mail over routes for which he had the contract.

Trade in Navajo crafts became more important after 1900 as tourism and interest in American Indians grew in Anglo-American society. Hubbell sold many rugs directly to visitors to his posts, but he also had a thriving mail order business. An artist who had benefited from his hospitality helped him design and publish a small, brochure-sized catalog. It was printed in Chicago and included some errors, but was used with good effect nonetheless. The wholesale market accounted for the greater part of his sales of Navajo textiles and probably of other crafts as well. Herman Schweizer, who headed the curio business of the Fred Harvey hotel chain, became a close friend and one of his best customers. Hubbell also experimented with placing goods on consignment with eastern stores, and having a traveling salesman take his goods to Indian stores in the major resort areas. He even briefly owned a retail store in Los Angeles devoted to the sale of Indian goods.

He kept many people employed. Some of these were relatives, including a brother, a son, a son-in-law, a daughter, and a cousin. Several

Lorenzo Hubbell, Jr., at Oraibi Trading Post, ca. 1904.

Don Lorenzo stands behind President William Howard Taft as he signs Arizona into statehood, 14 February 1912.

members of the Rubí and Armijo families who were related to Doña Lina also held responsible positions. Some worked as bookkeepers, managers of outlying posts, or clerks. Others served as freighters. Epimenio and Elias were the most prominent of the Armijos in his organization.

This tendency to give jobs to family members, especially key positions, contributed to the feudal flavor of his empire. Combined with his paternalistic attitude toward his customers, his hospitality, and his penchant for building on an ambitious scale, his example has led writers to apply titles to Hubbell such as "king" and to describe his lifestyle as "baronial." One anthropologist has characterized traders in general as "shoguns."

Don Lorenzo's influence in the wider world was most direct in politics. As a member of the Arizona Legislature, he was an advocate for women's right to vote, prohibition, and statehood, all of which became law during his lifetime. He also played an active role in supporting the rights of Hispanics in the state.

In less direct fashion, his hospitality influenced art, writing, and science. Stewart Culin's description of his visit in 1902 provides a graphic account of life in Don Lorenzo's home and of the quality of experience a visitor might have.

Mr. Hubbell himself is one of the most interesting characters on the Arizona frontier. Half Mexican by birth, he is a self-educated man. Of amazing courage, industry and intelligence, he is respected and feared by every man, American, Mexican, and Indian, on all the vast Navajo reservation. The Navajo travel a hundred miles to trade in his store; the Mexicans regard him as their best friend, and Americans, whether traders, artists, or investigator, find him ever the most cordial host in all this land of warm and unstinted hospitality. He keeps open house for everyone. All comers are welcome alike at his table.

Dining room of the
Hubbell home, ca. 1906

Mr. Hubbell retained many objects which his Mexican ancestors had brought three hundred years ago from Spain. Among them is a picture of the Holy Family, attributed to Correggio, which has been highly valued by artists who have seen it. My visit was enlivened by his many anecdotes of his early life on the border.

The family table was spread in the great hall at the new house. All ate together, host, Father Liopold, a Protestant missionary and his wife, Mr. Hubbell's son Lorencito, laborers and Mexicans. At the meals, Mr. Hubbell related his "summer stories." At night, all gathered about the big fireplace. Fritz, the German cook,

would sing German and student songs, an old Mexican,
Spanish cantarcitos, and we would eat jerked beef
cooked on the blazing coals.

Navajo rug designs
painted by Bertha A.
Little, ca. 1905, Hubbell
Collection.

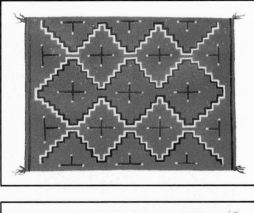

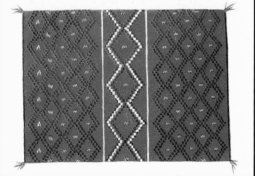

Don Lorenzo's hospitality also gave rise to his art collection, which largely consisted of works by numerous guest artists who wanted to paint Indians, Indian country, and similar subject matter. Many made their first visits as young artists still working to establish reputations in the art world. Those who succeeded doubtless felt grateful to Hubbell for simple hospitality, and many considered their visits important factors in their careers.

Eldridge Ayer Burbank, who traveled widely throughout the West in the 1890s, was perhaps the first to pay extended visits to Ganado. Some of his artwork bears the earliest dates of any in the Hubbell home, and certainly he contributed more to Hubbell's collection than any other artist. Burbank specialized in red Conté crayon portraits of Indians, and he also produced oil paintings. Unique to the Hubbell collection is a set of small paintings of Navajo rug designs. It is difficult to tell today which artworks were gifts from Burbank, and which were purchased by Don Lorenzo.

Several other guests added a few examples. Bertha A. Little's rug paintings are perhaps the most carefully done of all. Other artist visitors included Maynard Dixon and Joe J. Mora, both residents of San Francisco who gained fame as illustrators of the West. These and other artists became long-term friends of Don Lorenzo and corresponded with him for many years.

The artists' letters to Don Lorenzo show an easy familiarity, typical of the informality that Culin's description suggests of his stay at Ganado. Dixon and Mora were both in the San Francisco earthquake and fire of 1906 and wrote Hubbell to tell him of their experiences. Frank P. Sauerwein wrote

"The Weaver," oil painting by Maynard Dixon, ca. 1902, Hubbell Collection.

Maynard Dixon.

a far-from-complimentary description of El Centro, California, in 1910, full of humor and irony about the boosterism of the developers of that young community. Burbank's letters were usually short and not very informative, but he wrote frequently as he traveled from one reservation to another doing portraits.

"Chief Many Horses," red Conté crayon drawing by E.A. Burbank, ca. 1907, Hubbell Collection.

Artists often tried to sell Navajo rugs for Hubbell and arranged for framing art in his collection in places such as San Francisco and Chicago. They frequently owed him money as well, and would write to explain their financial troubles. Their artistic impulses led them to add illustrations at times; some sent hand-painted Christmas cards. Mora faithfully sent a personalized card each year to chronicle the growth of his family. The Hubbell Christmas card collection is a miniature art gallery in its own right.

The romance of Indian country attracted writers and lecturers, including Charles Lummis, who founded the Southwest Museum in Los Angeles, lecturer Frederick Monsen, writer Hamlin Garland, and George Wharton James, who promoted Hubbell's rugs in his book on Navajo weaving. Politicians, including Theodore Roosevelt, also visited. One of the most unusual attractions that Don Lorenzo could offer was a trip to the Hopi Snake Dance, and he often arranged far in advance to take parties to that ceremony.

Politics helped slow the pace Don Lorenzo set for himself. Doña Lina died in 1913, but this loss did not stop him from running for the United States Senate in 1914. His colleagues in the Republican Party urged him to enter the race. The party was split as a result of a falling out between President William Howard Taft and his predecessor in office, Teddy Roosevelt. Both ran for office in 1912, Taft as the candidate of his party and Roosevelt on a splinter ticket called the Bull Moose Party. This made victory easy for the Democratic candidate, Woodrow Wilson. The divisiveness of that campaign carried over to 1914, and Hubbell faced a difficult course. He borrowed heavily to finance his campaign. Despite all efforts and his own good record, he lost the election and was left burdened with a debt he could not pay off during his lifetime.

One of his major creditors was Henry Chee Dodge, a Navajo leader whose success in bridging the cultural gap between the Indian and non-Indian worlds had made him a wealthy man. As a close personal friend, Dodge did not press for quick payment, but he held a mortgage on much of Hubbell's property from that time on.

Former President Theodore Roosevelt (left), Don Lorenzo, and photographer at Walpi, Arizona, to observe Hopi Snake Dance, ca. 1913.

In 1914 a war broke out in Europe that would eventually involve the United States. Wilson's election, or perhaps more accurately the divided condition of the Republicans, left Don Lorenzo with far less political influence. His progressive philosophy allied him with many in the West who were abandoning the Republicans and giving their votes to the Democratic Party, but he remained loyal to his old associates.

The business world responded enthusiastically to the demands of the European conflict. Even with the burdens of debt, Hubbell was able to continue life at Ganado much as before. After the United States entered the war, wool and lambs commanded record prices.

Following the war, there was a brief period of inflation that exceeded the growth of Navajo income. The flu epidemic of 1918 was a major disaster. In the Southern Navajo Agency, which included Ganado, Navajo deaths from the disease ran about 6 percent of total population. A secondary effect of the epidemic was loss of livestock as the members of families were sometimes stricken simultaneously, leaving their herds uncared for until some recovered. Still, the 1920s were mostly years of greater prosperity, more due to increased rug weaving and wage work than to prices of wool and lambs.

Economic prosperity led to developments on the reservation that might not have taken place so soon in other circumstances. Roads were built and improved through much of the area. Automobiles and trucks soon began to replace carriages and wagons. Government and mission schools were built and increasing numbers of Navajo students attended.

After Doña Lina died, the house in Albuquerque was sold and the furniture was shipped to Ganado, where much of it remained in storage for years thereafter. The children made Ganado their family home. Adela and her husband Forest brought their two sons, Hubbell (Hub) and Miles (Mudgy) to live there. Two years after Barbara's husband was killed, she came to live at Ganado and raised her daughter, LaCharles (ChaCha), there. Lorenzo, Jr., looked to his father regularly for advice, and they cooperated in many business endeavors. Young Roman married a beautiful dancer, Alma Dorr, and took a job in southern Arizona for awhile, then moved to Gallup to run his father's store there. After Alma died in the flu epidemic of 1918, Roman moved to Ganado with his two sons, Roman (Monnie) and John (Jack).

Adela was seldom at Ganado in the 1920s, but Mudgy remained to attend the private school that the family began for the grandchildren. One of a series of teachers hired to run the school was Dorothy Smith. A year after her arrival she married Roman and became the stepmother who raised the boys. Other students in the school at different times included the children of George and Madge Hubbell and Epimenio Armijo's son, Rafael.

The family's propensity for nicknames was not restricted to the grandchildren. Adela was usually called Lala, Barbara was Auntie Bob, and Dorothy became Lady.

In the 1920s Don Lorenzo placed Roman in charge at Ganado and began to spend more time in Gallup. The family continued to plant the fields at Ganado, almost always losing money on the crop, but finding satisfaction

Grandchildren Hubbell Parker and LaCharles Goodman, ca. 1915.

in carrying on their agricultural tradition. The main crop was alfalfa hay, but some corn, rye, oats, and potatoes were grown. A garden yielded melons, tomatoes, and other delicacies. Numerous apple, pear, apricot, plum, and mulberry trees were planted along irrigation ditches. Grapes and black walnuts added variety. The harsh weather of the high country often ruined the fruit crop, especially for sensitive species such as apricots. Don Lorenzo also owned two bean farms south of Gallup and two apple orchards near Farmington. Even with these, his farming activities were more those of a country gentleman than those of a serious agriculturist. This was especially true after trucks replaced horse power for freighting in the mid-1920s. The value of the hay for Ganado was lost and other crops did not compensate for that loss.

Grandchildren Miles Parker and LaCharles Goodman watch departing freight wagons cross Ganado Wash, ca. 1915.

Grandchildren gave the old homestead a more domestic air than it had possessed earlier. Workers enjoyed the diversion they provided. Joe Borrego, the blacksmith, became their special friend, sometimes allowing them to pump the bellows for him. The great barn was their favorite playground. For them, it was a castle, a fortress, a pirate ship, a place for all the adventures and minor mishaps of childhood.

Grandfather Hubbell was very strict. The children were required to be at meals on time and could not get in the way of the workers, but they had free run of the place except for the blacksmith shop, where they could watch and help but not play. At times, they did get into trouble. They once raced their horses about in the fields, creating trampled paths in the alfalfa.

The old man like to tease the children, too. He would tell them that if they ran fast enough into the next room behind the mounted elk head then they might see the rest of the beast. They went as fast as they could, but they never caught the elk off guard. Don Lorenzo also would wake his

Miles Parker, LaCharles Goodman, Hubbell Parker, Forest Parker, Dolly Williams, Charolette Chain, and Adela Parker enjoy the Parker's new Locomobile, ca. 1915.

favorite grandchildren early and walk with them through the garden to find ripe melons.

Don Lorenzo's daughters took charge of the household with enthusiasm, softening the masculine atmosphere, despite their additional duties in the business. For many years, Barbara was the postmistress. Like the men, the Hubbell women would often help in the store during the busy seasons of wool and lamb buying. Dorothy also helped after marrying Roman.

Don Lorenzo continued to play host to all passersby as long as he stayed at Ganado. By 1920, however, his art collection was substantially complete and he was present far less often. In Gallup, it was not so easy, and more expensive, to treat visitors, whom he sometimes took to dinner at the El Navajo, the Harvey House Hotel by the railroad station.

The demands of the business became steadily greater. When he went to see his old friend, Cotton, to buy stock for the store, sell rugs or wool, or arrange an extension of his credit, he knew he must suffer yet another lecture on his business practices. Cotton would admonish Hubbell to pay less attention to politics and more to accounting, to be less generous when buying rugs, to supervise his workers more strictly, or to be more prompt in filling orders. Cotton, ever the consummate businessman, could not ignore a lapse, even in a longtime friend.

Chewing on his cigar with his gold-capped teeth, Cotton would complain that an order for two thousand goats was slow to arrive, or warn Hubbell that certain of his teamsters got drunk when they delivered freight in town. Hubbell did not like to put pressure on his Navajo employees to make prompt deliveries. Also, many of his teamsters were relatives through either his mother's or his wife's families; he would not fire them for drinking, however much he opposed the use of alcohol. Cotton was undoubtedly aware of the constraints of custom and family ties, but as the Hubbell business became more burdened with debt, he grew more earnest. Hubbell would have to endure the lecture, but Cotton could not deny the old partner of his youth and in the end would allow him more credit or time to fill an order.

Don Lorenzo in 1930, the year he died.

Lorenzo, Jr., acquired the Winslow store about 1920 from the Richardsons, a family of traders with numerous posts in the western part of Navajo country. For many years, he made Oraibi his headquarters. He was as noted for his hospitality as his father, and many a traveler to the Hopi villages and beyond was indebted to him for his kindness. Like his father, he could temper his acquisitive instincts to ensure the well-being of his Indian customers. He sponsored more Navajos as post managers than Don Lorenzo did.

Roman was more of a romantic than either his father or his brother. He could empathize with the Navajos' culture in ways that neither of the other two were able, but he was also less skilled as a trader. He was the only member of the family to have his own sweathouse, and participated in a Nightway ceremony in 1921. His Navajo friend, the singer Miguelito, or Red Point, believed that the ceremony might cure Roman's deafness. When Roman later found a hearing aid that improved his condition, the Navajos knew that the treatment had had an effect, for the ways of the gods were often mysterious and indirect.

Roman was more compatible with anthropologists than artists. In 1925 Gladys A. Reichard first visited Ganado, during research for her first

Lorenzo Hubbell, Jr., displays a Yeibichai rug at Oraibi Trading Post, ca. 1923.

major study of Navajo ways. She credited only anonymous traders in the resulting book on the tribe's social structure, but her later works invariably gave thanks to Roman by name and her monumental *Navaho Religion* was dedicated to him. While anthropologists have long found traders helpful intermediaries in their work with Indian people, few could match Roman's intimate knowledge of the most esoteric aspects of their customers' lives, nor his ability to share it with a professional student of the human experience.

As Don Lorenzo grew older and had less energy to oversee the business, profits declined. As one mortgage was paid off, another was needed, perhaps to refinance the first. By the late 1920s there were debts for delinquent taxes. Hubbell's health deteriorated, and in 1927 he came to live again at Ganado, where he could be cared for more easily.

Don Lorenzo liked to joke that Hubbell Hill, a knoll across the wash from his home, was "only an ant hill" when he first arrived, half a century earlier. In 1930 he died and was buried there alongside Doña Lina and his old Navajo friend, Many Horses.

Roman Hubbell at Ganado chicken pull, ca. 1915.

The Second Generation

Don Lorenzo bequeathed the business to his children. Roman was in charge, but Lorenzo, Jr., seems to have participated in most major decisions, and all four siblings were probably equal heirs to the estate.

Roman and Dorothy moved to Gallup, leaving Ganado under hired managers for many years. Roman began operating a tour service of Indian country, a necessary supplement to the declining revenues of the trading enterprise and the consistent losses of the farm as the Great Depression sapped the nation's economy.

To make matters worse, a severe blizzard struck in 1931 while Roman was holding over ten thousand lambs for market. Many lambs died, and by the time the weather cleared the season for selling was over. The losses that winter plunged the family deeper than ever into debt.

As Monnie and Jack grew up, Dorothy was able to devote more time to the business and proved an able overseer. She kept Roman's romantic views tethered to the realities of the business world.

Roman Hubbell conducting tours of Navajo country, ca. 1946.

Cotton retired the year Don Lorenzo died. His friendly, if stern, advice was not as readily available to the younger generation, nor did they have the kind of relationship that Don Lorenzo had enjoyed. There also was a degree of sibling rivalry between Roman and Lorenzo, Jr., that sometimes disrupted their joint efforts. But most crucial of all was the Depression itself, which had devastating effects on markets and prices. This was followed by the federal government's poorly coordinated programs to deal with the economic slump and the overgrazing of the Navajo range. A mandatory reduction of livestock impoverished the Navajos while the New Deal projects intended to provide the income to offset the loss of livestock were slow to materialize and were temporary palliatives, at best.

On the other hand, programs administered under the Indian Civilian

Conservation Corps (CCC–ID), the Works Progress Administration (WPA), and other agencies did contribute much-needed infrastructure such as schools, roads, bridges, irrigation systems, and erosion control.

Policies of the New Deal did recognize the validity and importance of native cultures. Anthropologists were hired to help gain a better understanding of the people. Gladys Reichard was assigned to teach Navajos how to read and write their own language in a "hogan school" established at Ganado, where her friendship with local leaders such as Red Point helped her work within the community. Ruth Underhill produced a book on Navajo history and culture for use in the schools. Clyde Kluckhohn, Dorothea and Alexander Leighton, and others wrote descriptions of Navajo society and culture to guide bureaucrats in their work.

Unfortunately, this sensitivity to the ways of the local people was not shared by all. Many older government employees, missionaries, traders, and even Navajos trained in the strict assimilationist schools of the past opposed the new policies and resisted their implementation. Those who promoted the changes were often the same people who advocated and, in some instances, carried out stock reduction, a program that struck at the very heart of the Navajo way of life. The purchase and slaughter of Navajo sheep and goats horrified Navajos dependent on their herds.

Navajo grudgingly comply with federally mandated livestock reduction, ca. 1934.

Incongruity of the two policies did not seem to be recognized by those involved, so strong was their dedication to recognition of the dignity of Indian ways on the one hand, and to conservation on the other. The result, quite naturally, was political turmoil on a grand scale.

For the traders, the ultimate source of their income—the sheep herds—were being attacked by the government. Most Depression-era government jobs were best suited to the skills of younger Navajos, not those of the more mature generation who had controlled family income through their traditional control of the herds. Traders used to dealing with hard assets were reluctant to advance credit to Navajo families on the basis of paychecks given to the workers, and demanded that pay be channeled through the trading posts. At first, the Indian Service willingly acceded to this request in order to keep the Navajos eligible for credit, but abuses by some traders led to renewed contention.

Roman was among the traders who advocated delivery of pay to the traders. He and Lorenzo, Jr., both wrote lengthy letters to government officials setting forth the traders' arguments in favor of their position. Meanwhile, dwindling income and constant payments on the mortgage put a severe strain on the entire family.

Facing Page: The Bull Pen today.

The Bull Pen at Hubbell Trading Post, ca. 1949.

The old homestead, even when occupied by hired help, had an emotional value far beyond what it represented as an investment. So, despite the Depression, construction at Ganado continued. A modern guest hogan with electricity and plumbing was built near the wash, not for overnight stays by Navajo customers but for visitors and business travelers. A Mexican mason cut the stones, but quit to return to Mexico before the job was done. The building was originally planned to have a full masonry dome roof, which would have quickly collapsed on the unstable soil of the valley. A more modest, lightweight frame roof allowed this memorial to their father to serve the second generation as long as the property remained in the family.

World War II brought new opportunity to revive the family fortunes, but also called the young men to serve. LaCharles' husband, Edward Eckel, went to Europe and Monnie went to the Pacific. Monnie, regarded as the likely heir to the Indian trading tradition of the family, was killed on Manus Island in 1943.

Employees occupied the house and, in one case, converted it for use as a place for paying guests to stay. They uncrated the opulent furniture

brought from the Albuquerque home and installed it in what had been the workers' dining room. So great was the elegance of this setting that one could easily imagine Don Lorenzo hosting a distinguished roster of guests. This mystique undoubtedly enchanted tourists who came to stay, but obscured the true history of the old home.

Adela, who had not lived at Ganado since the mid–1920s, died in 1938. Lorenzo, Jr., died in 1942. On a cold, cloudy day, his body was carried to the top of Hubbell Hill to rest beside his parents. Roman and Dorothy, along with Barbara, were left with both branches of the family business. The three moved to Winslow not long after Lorenzo's death and ran the businesses from the Winslow store until 1953, when debt became too much for them to handle. They returned to Ganado and declared bankruptcy in 1954, a painful experience that led to the loss of most of their holdings except the Ganado property. The old homestead was their tie to the past and link to the beginnings of the family's trading days, their last home in Navajo country as it had been their first.

Roman died in 1957 and Barbara moved to Denver to spend her last years with her daughter. Dorothy carried on alone at Ganado, hiring managers for the store. Many Navajos remained loyal customers through all the comings and goings, even bringing long-hoarded tin money to spend.

By the 1960s most trading posts were converting to self-service. A convenience store opened in Ganado, and supermarkets in the reservation border towns offered a strong pull with low prices and a great variety of goods. But the past lived on at Hubbell Trading Post, where business followed the old patterns. Clerks behind the counters filled orders for customers, did business in the Navajo language, and gave credit for pawned jewelry. In the house, Dorothy kept most of the furnishings intact, living among the collected mementos of a well-remembered time when the Hubbell store *was* Ganado.

Dorothy was aware of the historic values of the post, but there was no one in the family prepared to continue the trading tradition. Finally, in 1967, the National Park Service undertook to preserve the site. It did not come to the government easily, however. There was opposition in Congress to the purchase of the property. The efforts of Dr. Edward B. Danson, director of the Museum of Northern Arizona in Flagstaff, were the key to success, for only the word of an eminent scholar could overcome the doubts that the old trading post had true historic values, bringing long-delayed recognition to the role of the reservation trader in Native American history.

Amid the political activism of the 1960s, abuses prevalent among some of the traders in Navajo country were widely publicized. It is noteworthy that Navajos involved in this reform movement cited the example of Don Lorenzo as a good trader, an ideal that they hoped traders of their day might emulate. His memory remained untarnished among the older Navajos who had traded with him, and was passed on to their grandchildren, who hoped to gain fairer treatment for their people in dealings with the outsiders.

The Jewelry Room, Hubbell Trading Post National Historic Site.

Epilogue ~ View from the Hogan

To the Navajos, traders were intruders—aliens who came and settled, usually uninvited and often at choice spots, to exchange goods from eastern farms and factories for whatever Indians had to offer.

Hubbell was more qualified, and welcome, than most traders. He spoke English and Spanish, and was beginning to learn Navajo as well. While working for the Navajo agency, he had come to know the two most important headmen: Manuelito, variously leader of the eastern Navajos and the entire tribe, and Ganado Mucho, usually regarded as leader of the western Navajos. Both leaders trusted Hubbell and believed he, being a younger man, would respect them on the basis of age at least, if not for their status among their people. It is perhaps no accident that Hubbell's first two trading locations were near the homes of these two headman.

In his youth, Manuelito won a heroic victory over a Mexican army invading Navajo country. He seemed to be blessed with supernatural powers, and won many battles thereafter until the disaster of the final Navajo wars. He was dubbed Holy Boy as a result, while his war name, Hashké Naabaah, "Angry Warrior," was well-earned in battle. He is remembered better by the name he gained from the place where he lived as an old man, Hastiin Ch'il Haajiní, "Mr. Black Plants."

Manuelito was a man of great intelligence, charisma, and courage. He held out longer than any other leading Navajo headman as Carson's troops scourged Navajoland. He surrendered only when wounded, his wealth destroyed, and his followers dispersed. In defeat, he was quick to realize the need to accommodate to this new power in the Southwest.

Facing Page: Don Lorenzo and Navajo weaver at Hubbell Trading Post, ca. 1890.

He led the first Indian police force organized by the federal government, which successfully prevented renewed warfare after the Navajos returned from exile. He supported the establishment of boarding schools, even though this meant long separations between parents and children that raised memories of Navajo women and children being kidnapped and sold into slavery. Manuelito himself lost two sons, who died at an Indian school in Pennsylvania.

While he could accept defeat intellectually and adapt to it intelligently, he never accepted it in his heart. He was eloquent in objecting to injustice, in opposing agents who did not try to help Navajos, and in expressing feelings of helplessness that the final wars had brought about.

Ganado Mucho was very different. Short in stature, a heritage of his Puebloan ancestry, he was known as Tótsohnii Hastiin, "Man of the Big Water Clan." He was an effective leader who brought his people back from Fort Sumner to establish farms along the Pueblo Colorado Wash. He appears to have given Hubbell full support as a trader. Hubbell later honored Ganado Mucho by submitting the community name Ganado, rather than Pueblo Colorado, to postal authorities, thus avoiding confusion with the Colorado town named Pueblo. Hubbell's closest Navajo friend was one of Ganado Mucho's sons, Many Horses, a man more nearly his own age.

Hubbell's trading career at Ganado lasted over half a century. He may have acquired a Navajo name, no longer remembered, when he first came to the valley. For many years his name—Nák´ee Sinilí—was based on his wearing eyeglasses. Ultimately, he was known simply as Naakaii Sání, "Old Mexican."

All older Navajos in Ganado in the 1970s agreed that Naakaii Sání had helped them survive the difficult years of the late nineteenth and early twentieth centuries. Many Navajo families were impoverished even during the years of greater prosperity. At Naakaii Sání's trading post they could find sympathy, credit, and sometimes even direct assistance. He would not turn away a blanket or rug, even a poor one, without offering to purchase it, giving as good a price as any trader, and often better. Navajos did not like to haggle over prices, and found Naakaii Sání's trading overall to be fair.

Naakaii Sání touched the lives of all the people of the Valley of the Red House, usually for the better. From at least the days of Ganado Mucho, Ganado has been a community where outstanding people could make their mark. Many local people have achieved notable success. Many Horses' leadership in agricultural work is still remembered today. Red Point was a singer able to communicate to outsiders the dignity and beauty that lies at the heart of Navajo religion. Maria Antonia, Red Point's wife, inspired Gladys Reichard to write of the strength and abilities of Navajo women. The valley's weavers and silversmiths—notably Elle of Ganado, David H. Taliman, and Luke B. Yazzie—often went on to a larger stage.

Political leadership has always been strong. Henry Taliman served as chairman of the Navajo Tribal Council in 1937-38, and Howard Gorman served as vice chairman from 1938 to 1942. Gorman's wit and wisdom is honored with an exhibit hall at the tribal fairgrounds that bears his name. During the 1960s and 1970s, Deescheeny Nez Tracy was elder statesman for the young activists seeking to ensure that self-determination became a reality. Finally, two men of Ganado have served in the Arizona State Senate. The first was Naakaii Sání; the second, many years later, was Arthur J. Hubbard, Sr., who defended Navajo interests for several terms.

Navajos found in Naakaii Sání a white man who in many ways embodied the ideals they expected in their own leaders: good humor, energy, personal success, and, above all, generosity. What he built did not remain intact beyond his lifetime, but this was not a failing from the Navajo point of view. What has lasted is the goodwill that he engendered, a source of belief that it is possible for people of different races, languages, and cultures to live and work together in harmony, if only they try. Hubbell Trading Post National Historic Site strives to keep that spirit alive.

Other National Parks to Visit

Acknowledgments

I am indebted to many whose work and help I must acknowledge. My former Navajo tribal colleagues, J. Lee Correll and Martin A. Link, were ever helpful during my five years as curator at Hubbell Trading Post.

Scholars who stoked my desire to learn more were Frank McNitt, Charlotte J. Frisbie, Stephen C. Jett, Donald L. Parman, Joe Ben Wheat, and Leland C. Wyman. Dorothy Hubbell and La Charles Eckel provided key insights about life there, while Phillip Hubbell introduced me to the Hubbell home in Pajarito. I must give special credit to Charles Colley, Victoria Best, and Clinton Colby for their work with the Hubbell papers.

Most important were the stories and memories of the local people and their help in broadening my understanding of Navajo lifeways. Those whose friendship and help were the most significant include Arthur J. Hubbard, Sr., Howard Gorman, Clarence Brown, Friday Kinlcheenie, and Roberta Tso, to whom this work is dedicated.

To all whom I cannot include here, you are not forgotten, and you have my thanks as well.

D.M.B.

Suggested Reading

Bailey, Garrick and Robert Glenn Bailey, *A History of the Navajos: The Reservation Years*, Santa Fe, N. Mex.: School of American Research Press, 1986.

Fontana, Bernard L., ed., *Querido Patron—Letters from Maynard Dixon to Lorenzo Hubbell*, Tucson, Ariz.: Friends of the University of Arizona Library, 1987.

Hoffman, Virginia, ed., *Navajo Biographies, Volume I*, Rough Rock, Ariz.: Navajo Curriculum Center Press, 1974.

Johnson, Broderick H., ed., *Stories of Traditional Navajo Life and Culture by Twenty-two Navajo Men and Women*, Tsaile, Ariz.: Navajo Community College Press, 1977.

Reichard, Gladys A., *Navaho Medicine Man, Sandpaintings and Legends of Miguelito*. New York, N.Y.: J. J. Augustin, 1939.

Roberts, Willow, *Stokes Carson: Twentieth-Century Trading on the Navajo Reservation*, Albuquerque, N. Mex.: University of New Mexico Press, 1987.

Williams, Lester L., *C. N. Cotton and His Navaho Blankets*, Albuquerque, N. Mex.: Awanyu Publishing Inc., 1989.